KRABI

TRAVEL GUIDE 2024

ALICE JOHN

Contents

Introduction to Krabi

Oh, where do I even begin? Picture this: a hidden gem situated in the embrace of Thailand, a place where the whispers of the Andaman Sea gently meet the rugged whispers of towering limestone cliffs. This, my friends, is Krabi—a paradise that unfolds like a well-kept secret, eager to be discovered by those who dare to venture beyond the ordinary.

I remember stepping off the plane, the warm, tropical air greeting me like an old friend, wrapping me in its comforting embrace. It was as if Krabi itself was extending a welcoming hand, inviting me into its treasure trove of wonders. And oh, what wonders they were! From the emerald waters of the Phi Phi Islands, where the ocean seemed to hold the sky in a loving embrace, to the sacred tranquility of the Tiger Cave Temple, perched atop a stairway that challenges both body and spirit, each step a testament to the pilgrim's resolve.

But let me tell you, the beauty of Krabi isn't just in its postcard-perfect landscapes. No, it's in the rhythm of life itself—the bustling night markets in Ao Nang, where the air is thick with the tantalizing aromas of Thai delicacies, each bite a burst of flavor, a celebration of the rich culinary tapestry that is Thai cuisine. It's in the laughter of the locals, whose warmth and hospitality are as inviting as the cool waters of Railay Beach, a haven for adventurers and dreamers alike.

And the adventures, oh, they are endless! From kayaking through the serene waters of the mangrove forests, where silence is a language spoken by the rustling leaves and the gentle lapping of water against the kayak, to the exhilarating climb up to the viewpoint on Railay, where the world seems to stretch out endlessly before you, a canvas painted with hues of blue and green so vivid, they seem almost surreal.

As I share this story with you, I can't help but feel a surge of joy, a longing to return to that magical place where every sunset felt like a promise of a new dawn. Krabi, with its enchanting beauty, its vibrant culture, and its unspoiled landscapes, is not just a destination; it's a journey, a journey that beckons to the soul, urging it to explore, to discover, and ultimately, to fall in love.

So, to those intending to visit Krabi, prepare yourselves. You're not just embarking on a trip; you're about to embark on an adventure of a lifetime, a story that you'll be eager to tell, just as I am now. Welcome to Krabi, the heart of Thailand's natural wonder.

Planning Your Trip to Krabi

Best Time to Visit

Best Time for Sunshine and Blue Skies

Ideal Months: December through April marks the best period to visit Krabi for those seeking sunny days and clear skies. This period is perfect for beach activities, island hopping, and exploring the natural beauty of Krabi without the interruption of rain.

Transitional Weather

Months of May and November: These months serve as a transitional period where the weather can be a bit unpredictable. While you can still enjoy warm temperatures and many sunny days, there's a higher chance of occasional rain showers. This time can still be suitable for visiting, especially if you prefer to avoid the peak tourist season and don't mind a bit of rain.

Rainy Season Insights

Low Season (June to October): The official rainy season in Krabi spans from June to October. This period is characterized by regular rain, typically in the form of short, heavy showers rather than continuous rain. Despite the rainfall, this season offers its own advantages, including fewer tourists, lower prices, and the lush, green landscapes that come alive with the rain.

Tips for Visiting Krabi

Flexibility During Transition Months: If you're visiting during May or November, it's wise to plan a flexible itinerary that can accommodate changes due to weather conditions.

Enjoying the Rainy Season: The rainy season can still be a great time to visit for those who enjoy the serenity of less crowded attractions and don't mind getting a bit wet. The rain often comes in short bursts, leaving plenty of dry spells to explore the area.

Activities for Every Season: Regardless of when you visit, Krabi offers a range of activities. During the dry season, beach and water activities are popular, while the cooler, wetter months are perfect for exploring waterfalls and the lush interior landscapes.

Accommodation and Flights: Consider booking your accommodation and flights well in advance if you're planning to visit during the peak season (December to April) to ensure availability and possibly secure better rates.

By choosing the right time for your visit based on your preferences and the activities you're most interested in, you can enjoy the best of what Krabi has to offer, whether it's basking in the sunshine on its beautiful beaches or enjoying the natural beauty during the greener, quieter rainy season.

Visa and Entry Requirements

Gaining entry into Thailand is straightforward for many international visitors thanks to the Visa on Arrival or Visa Exemption policies, which permit stays of either 30 or 45 days for tourists. It's essential to understand that tourists are individuals visiting for leisure and are not permitted to engage in work or business activities during their stay. Those with intentions other than tourism must explore alternative visa categories.

Understanding the Thailand Tourist Visa

The Thailand Tourist Visa is an official endorsement in your passport, facilitating your entry into Thailand for leisure purposes. This visa is obtained from a Thai embassy or Consulate prior to arrival and is stamped into your passport at a Thai airport. For those wishing to extend their stay, it's possible to apply for an extension once in Thailand. It's crucial not to confuse this visa with the Visa Exemption stamp received upon arrival.

Thailand offers both single-entry and multiple-entry tourist visas, catering to different travel plans:

Single-Entry Tourist Visa

Validity: Must be used to enter Thailand within 3 months from its issuance date.

Duration: Permits a stay of up to 60 days after entering Thailand.

Extension: An additional 30-day stay extension is available, totaling up to 90 days, subject to application at a Thai immigration office.

Multiple-Entry Tourist Visa

Validity: Grants multiple entries over 6 months from issuance.

Duration: Each entry allows a 60-day visit, with multiple entries permitted within the 6 months, each visit capped at 60 days.

Extension: Similar to the single-entry visa, a 30-day extension per entry is possible.

Requirements for a Thailand Tourist Visa

Necessary Documentation:

- ❖ A passport or similar travel document with at least 6 months validity remaining
- ❖ Completed visa application form
- ❖ 1 recent photograph of the applicant (4 x 6 cm)
- ❖ Confirmed round-trip ticket
- ❖ Evidence of sufficient funds (10,000 baht for individuals, 20,000 baht for families)

Accommodation confirmation

Consular Officers may ask for further documentation as needed. Given the current surge in applications post-Covid, it's wise to apply well in advance of your trip.

Visa Fee:

A fee of US $30.00 (or its equivalent) per entry is applicable. This fee is subject to change, hence checking with the nearest Thai Embassy or Consulate is advised.

In some countries, it's possible to apply for a Thailand tourist visa online. Verify with your local Thai Embassy whether in-person applications are required.

Length of Stay:

The tourist visa typically allows a 60-day visit, extendable by another 30 days at a local immigration office. The Special Tourist Visa (STV) offers up to a 9-month stay, available until September 2022, subject to specific requirements.

This overview should assist in navigating the process of securing a tourist visa for Thailand, ensuring a smooth entry for leisure travel.

Map

Once scanned, the QR code will reveal an interactive map tailored to your guide

scan here

For Step by Step on how to do, go to the next page

Unlock Interactive Exploration

Step 1: Get Your Device Ready
- Ensure your smartphone or tablet is equipped with a QR code scanner app. If you don't have one, simply download a free QR code scanner from your device's app store.

Step 2: Locate the QR Code
- Turn to the designated page in your "Krabi Travel Guide 2024" to find the QR code. It's your key to unlocking an interactive map experience.

Step 3: Open the QR Code Scanner
- Launch your QR code scanner app and point your device's camera at the QR code. Make sure the entire code is within the frame, and your device will automatically recognize it.

Step 4: Explore in Real-Time
- Once scanned, the QR code will reveal an interactive map tailored to your guide. Explore attractions, hidden gems, and local insights right from your device. Zoom in, tap on icons, and dive into the beauty of Krabi.

Step 5: Enhance Your Journey
- Immerse yourself in a richer travel experience. Discover detailed information, get real-time updates, and access exclusive content linked to the locations in your guide.

Step 6: Enjoy Your Adventure!
- Embark on a seamless journey through Krabi with the power of technology at your fingertips. Make the most of your travel guide's QR code for an unforgettable exploration.

Note: Internet connectivity may be required for certain features. Ensure you have a stable connection for the best interactive experience.

Getting to Krabi

By Aircraft: Direct flights are available to Krabi from Singapore with Tiger Airways (80060-15637; www.tigerairways.com). Suvarnabhumi International Airport outside Bangkok serves as the hub for Thai Airways (tel. 02356-1111; www.thaiair.com), Bangkok Airways (tel. 02270-6699; www.bangkokair.com), and AirAsia (tel. 02515-9999; www.airasia.com).

From Krabi airport, you can take a minivan to the town for 90B, or pay more for destinations further away. Cab fares start at 350B.

By Boat: Boats leave Ko Phi Phi for Krabi at 9 a.m., 10:30 a.m., 1:30 p.m., and 3 p.m.; the trip takes 90 minutes and costs 350B. In the high season, there is only one boat departing from Ko Lanta at 11:30 a.m., which takes two hours and costs 400B. During the rainy season, visitors must take a minivan, which takes two hours and costs between 250B to 300B, with many departures available.

Via Minivan or Bus: Two air-conditioned VIP 24-seat buses leave daily for Krabi Town from Bangkok's Southern Bus Terminal (tel. 02422-4444; fare: 970B; journey duration: 12 hours). Air-conditioned minibuses operate on a regular schedule from Surat Thani to Krabi daily (2:45 hours; 250B). Air-conditioned minivans also leave from Phuket Town to Krabi every day (journey duration: 3 hours; cost: 140B).

Visitor Information

In Krabi town, Utarakit Road, which runs parallel to the shoreline, hosts the majority of services (on the right as you disembark from the boat). Here, you will find the TAT Office (07562-2163) and several banks with ATM services. Turn left as you leave the dock to locate the police station and post office (tel. 07563-7208), situated south on Utarakit Road. Krabi Nakharin International Hospital is located on Pisanpob Road in the northwest of the town and can be reached at www.krabinakharin.co.th or by phone at 07562-6555.

A free local map, showing the resort area, town, and nearby islands, is available at small businesses around the town.

Navigating

Krabi Town is the area's commercial center, though not many choose to reside there. Songthaews (pickup trucks) frequently run between Krabi Town and Ao Nang Beach; simply hail a white pickup for the 30-minute, 30-B ride.

Boat transport is required to reach Railay Beach and the resorts on nearby beaches due to a range of cliffs separating them from the mainland. Fares start at 100B from the Krabi Town dock for the 45-minute journey. From Ao Nang beach (at the small pavilion opposite the Phra Nang Inn), it takes about 20 minutes and costs 80B.

Khlong Muang beach is about 25 kilometers (16 miles) northwest of Krabi Town. A cab ride there should cost at least 300B.

The limestone formations along this stretch of coastline are not only stunning to view but also provide excellent opportunities for small boat exploration. Some, like the renowned Ko Hong, are almost entirely enclosed, featuring dazzling blue lagoons at their centers. At low tide, boats navigate through small, nearly invisible openings to enter them; inquire about boat trips at your resort.

When checking into any resort, be sure to inquire about the weather and transportation plans, which are often included.

Accommodation Options in Krabi

Luxury Hotels

1) Anana Ecological Resort

Boasting 5-star accommodations, Anana Ecological Resort Krabi - SHA Extra Plus is located in Ao Nang Beach, 2.1 miles from Ao Nang Krabi Boxing Stadium and 5.6 miles from Dragon Crest Mountain. The resort offers a 24-hour front desk, room service, and luggage storage for guests. Complimentary WiFi is accessible throughout the property.

Each unit at the hotel is furnished with a seating area, a mini-bar, and a flat-screen TV. The private bathrooms are equipped with free environment-friendly toiletries, and selected rooms feature a terrace. All rooms include a desk.

Guests can enjoy an outdoor pool at Anana Ecological Resort Krabi.

Krua Thara Seafood Restaurant is 3.1 miles from the property, while Ao Phai Plong is 1.2 miles away. Krabi International Airport is 11 miles from the resort, with Tuk Tuk shuttle services available upon request.

Location: Ao Nanang, 81140 Ao Nang Beach, Thailand

Price: From $244 per night

2) Holiday Ao Nang Beach Resort

Positioned on the coast of Thailand, Holiday Ao Nang Beach Resort, Krabi - SHA Extra Plus Certified, offers a stunning boutique resort experience on the white sands of Ao Nang Beach. The resort features rooms that open directly onto a large freeform pool.

Located within breathtaking tropical landscaped grounds, the resort provides luxurious rooms with private terraces. The rooms are equipped with a DVD player, an elegant bathroom, and WiFi access.

Guests can spend a serene day at sea by renting a yacht or relax with a swim in the swimming pool.

InnAsia, the hotel's rooftop restaurant, offers fresh seafood and authentic Thai cuisine. The Wave Restaurant & Bar presents a selection of refreshing beverages and spectacular beach views.

Location: 123 Moo 3, Ao Nang, Muang, Krabi - 81180 Ao Nang Beach, Thailand

Price: From $127

Best Resorts for Couples

1) Phanom Bencha Mountain Resort

Located among tropical gardens, Phanom Bencha Mountain Resort offers intimate bungalows with mountain vistas. Guests can enjoy an outdoor pool and parking facilities. The resort organizes all-day and half-day treks.

Accessibility

- ❖ 15-minute drive from Tiger Cave Temple
- ❖ 20-minute ride from Krabi Airport and Bus Terminal

- ❖ 50-minute ride to Ao Nang Beach

Features

- ❖ Private balconies in bungalows
- ❖ Fan and an en-suite bathroom
- ❖ Complimentary toiletries

Dining

- ❖ Thai and Western dishes at Phanom Bencha Mountain Restaurant

Location: 42/2 Krabi Noi Moo.7, 81000 Krabi, Thailand

Price: From $25+ per night

2) The Fong Krabi Resort

The Fong Krabi Resort, located a convenient 15-minute drive to Aonang Beach and Krabi Town, provides air-conditioned rooms with balconies, free Wi-Fi, a tour desk, and free private parking.

Accessibility

- ❖ 20-minute drive from Krabi Airport
- ❖ Phi Phi Island is an hour by boat

Features

❖ Flat-screen cable TV and refrigerator

❖ Private bathroom with shower

❖ Welcome fruit set

Dining

❖ Breakfast and a la carte menu at I am Cafe (2-minute walk)

❖ Additional local dining within a 10-minute drive

Location: 27/5 Wachara Rd., Paknam, Muang, 81000 Krabi, Thailand

Price: $30

3) Islanda Hideaway Resort

Islanda Hideaway Resort - SHA Extra Plus offers serene beachfront accommodations on Klang Island, accessible via a 15-minute land transfer to Boat Lagoon and a 10-minute boat ride to the island. The resort features free WiFi, an outdoor infinity-edge pool, and a restaurant.

Accessibility

❖ Approximately 9.3 miles from Krabi International Airport

❖ Chargeable transfers from Krabi Town and Airport

Features:

❖ Spacious rooms with air-conditioning

❖ Open-air bathrooms

❖ Flat-screen satellite TVs and DVD players

Activities

❖ Batik painting and rice farming classes

❖ Day trips arrangement

Dining

❖ Thai and international cuisine at Sea Breeze Restaurant

❖ In-room dining option

Popularity

❖ Highly rated by solo travelers

Location: 177 Moo 3 T. Klong Prasong, Klang Island, A. Muang, Ko Klang, 81000 Krabi, Thailand

Price: From $90 per night

4) Krabi Boat Lagoon Resort

Located in Nue Khlong, Krabi Boat Lagoon Resort offers guests an idyllic retreat with an outdoor pool and a sun terrace. It's a haven for those seeking tranquility and convenience in the Krabi Province.

Key Features

- Air-conditioned accommodations with seating areas and private bathrooms
- Select units feature a dining area and/or a balcony
- Kitchenette equipped with a fridge and basic cooking appliances
- Free WiFi and private parking on-site
- On-site restaurant for dining convenience
- Bike hire available for exploring the surroundings
- Popular activities include cycling and canoeing

Accessibility

- Thara Park: 19 mi away
- Krabi pier - Klong Jirad: 17 mi away
- Pakasai Golf course: 6.2 mi away

- ❖ Krabi Airport: 9.3 mi away, ensuring easy access for travelers

Location: 178 Moo.2 Ban Klongsai, Talingchan, A.Nuea Khlong, 81130 Krabi, Thailand

Price: From $66 per night

5) VARANA Hotel Krabi

VARANA Hotel Krabi, located a short 5-minute walk from Koh Kwang Beach, offers world-class service with luxurious accommodations, making it an ideal choice for travelers seeking comfort and elegance.

Key Features

- ❖ Air-conditioned rooms with amenities such as a closet, coffee machine, fridge, minibar, safety deposit box, flat-screen TV, and balcony
- ❖ Private bathrooms equipped with showers
- ❖ Selected rooms feature a patio and/or sea views
- ❖ Free bikes, private parking, outdoor swimming pool, fitness center, garden, sauna, and hot tub
- ❖ 24-hour front desk, airport transportation, room service, and free WiFi throughout the property

* Breakfast options include à la carte, buffet, and continental
* 5-star accommodations with a hammam and terrace
* Activities like canoeing and cycling available for guests

Nearby Attractions:

Klong Muang Beach: 9-minute walk

Laem Bong Beach: 1.2 miles away

Krabi International Airport: 19 miles away

Location: 258 Moo 3 Tambol Nongtalay Amphur Muang Krabi 81180, Thailand, 81180 Klong Muang Beach

Both Krabi Boat Lagoon Resort and VARANA Hotel Krabi offer unique experiences for visitors to Krabi, catering to different preferences whether you're looking for a serene lagoon-side stay or a luxurious beachside holiday.

Top Affordable Family Hotels

Discover some of the best places for families to stay without breaking the bank during your visit to Krabi town, Thailand. Each hotel offers unique amenities to cater to both adults and children, ensuring a comfortable and enjoyable stay.

1) Play Poshtel & Cafe

Situated in Krabi town, merely 2.7 km away from Wat Kaew Korawaram, Play Poshtel & Cafe offers a blend of cozy accommodations and vibrant social spaces. This 4-

star establishment is equipped with complimentary bicycles, private parking, a serene garden, and a communal lounge. Benefiting from a round-the-clock front desk and concierge services, guests also enjoy complimentary Wi-Fi. The onsite restaurant serves a mix of American and Chinese cuisine, while the bar is perfect for evening cocktails.

Select rooms come with a kitchenette, including a microwave, ensuring all rooms are furnished with fresh bed linen and towels.

Breakfast is an à la carte affair, with American options to kickstart your day.

Distance to Attractions

❖ Thara Park: 3.9 km
❖ Krabi Stadium: 4.4 km
❖ Krabi International Airport: 10 km

Location: 66/6 Panurat, Pak Nam, Amphoe Mueang Krabi, 81000 Krabi town, Thailand

Starting Price: $15 per night

2) Family Tree Hotel

A stone's throw from Wat Kaew Korawaram (400m) and close to Thara Park (1.5km), Family Tree Hotel is a sanctuary in Krabi town. It offers comprehensive services including room service, concierge, free Wi-Fi, airport transfers, and bicycle rentals.

Rooms are air-conditioned and well-equipped with modern amenities such as a coffee machine, fridge, minibar, and flat-screen TV. Selected rooms also feature a balcony, and all are equipped with a kettle.

The hotel's restaurant serves a delightful mix of American, Chinese, and Thai dishes, with special diet menus available on request.

Distance to Attractions

- Krabi Stadium: 6.4 km
- Wat Tham Sua - Tiger Cave Temple: 9 km
- Krabi International Airport: 12 km

Location: 6 Maharaj Soi.2 Rd., Paknam, Mueang, Krabi, 81000 Krabi town, Thailand

Starting Price: $75 per night

3) The Brown Hotel

A short walk from Wat Kaew Korawaram and within easy reach of Thara Park, The Brown Hotel offers 3-star accommodations with a personal touch. Guests can enjoy free Wi-Fi in air-conditioned comfort, with private bathrooms. The hotel features a shared lounge, a terrace, and 24-hour front desk service.

Rooms are equipped with an electric kettle, flat-screen TV, and safety deposit box, with selected rooms offering balconies and city views. A fridge is standard in all guest rooms.

Distance to Attractions

❖ Krabi Stadium: 6 km
❖ Wat Tham Sua - Tiger Cave Temple: 8.5 km
❖ Krabi International Airport: 12 km

Location: 50-52, Maharaj 10 Road, Paknam, Mueang, 81000 Krabi, Thailand

Starting Price: $60 per night

4) The Seens Hotel

Situated just 1.2 miles from Wat Kaew Korawaram, The Seens Hotel is a charming retreat offering an array of amenities including an outdoor swimming pool, complimentary private parking, and a terrace. This 3-star hotel enhances your stay with free WiFi, a kids' club, and a helpful tour desk. Additional services such as luggage storage and currency exchange are also available to guests.

Rooms at The Seens Hotel are designed for comfort, featuring air conditioning, a desk, electric kettle, fridge, safety deposit box, flat-screen TV, and a private bathroom with a shower. Guests are also provided with fresh bed linen and towels.

Breakfast options include both buffet and Asian cuisine, ensuring a delightful start to your day.

Distance to Attractions

- ❖ Thara Park: 1.9 miles
- ❖ Krabi Stadium: 2.8 miles
- ❖ Krabi International Airport: 6.2 miles

Location: 316 Thanon Utarakit, Krabi Town, 81000 Krabi, Thailand

Starting Price: $41 per night

5) The Ozone Krabi Condote

The Ozone Krabi Condotel, located a bit further from the hustle and bustle, 2.9 miles from Wat Kaew Korawaram and 3.4 miles from Thara Park, offers a serene escape with modern conveniences. This property boasts a rooftop pool, complimentary WiFi, and private parking. Guests can also enjoy an indoor pool, a fitness center, and the convenience of an elevator.

Select units feature a terrace with sea views, a satellite flat-screen TV, and air conditioning. The apartment complex offers allergy-free and soundproof units for added comfort.

For dining in, a barbecue facility is available, and families will appreciate the baby safety gate feature for added security.

Distance to Attractions

- ❖ Krabi Stadium: 3.5 miles
- ❖ Wat Tham Sua - Tiger Cave Temple: 5.1 miles
- ❖ Krabi International Airport: 6.8 miles

Location: 195, Pak Nam, Muang, Krabi, 81000 Krabi, Thailand

Starting Price: $28+ per night

Both The Seens Hotel and The Ozone Krabi Condotel provide pleasant, cost-effective options for your stay in Krabi, ensuring a memorable and comfortable visit.

Exploring Krabi Town

Krabi Town, the heart of Krabi Province, presents a fascinating blend of attractions, from historical sites and natural wonders to a vibrant market life. Unlike the typical seaside resort towns, Krabi Town is situated along the serene Krabi River, offering a unique charm that attracts backpackers, long-term voyagers, and those looking to immerse themselves in a more authentic Thai experience. Affordable accommodation and a strategic location make it an ideal base for exploring Krabi's myriad attractions.

Why Krabi Town Stands Out

Unique Location: Nestled not by the sea but by the Krabi River, the town offers a distinct vibe from the coastal tourist spots, making it a haven for travelers seeking a more grounded experience.

Accommodation: Krabi Town excels in providing budget-friendly options, from chic boutique hotels like the Family Tree Hotel in the old town to backpacker-friendly choices such as the Sleep Well Hostel.

Travel Tips

Beach Proximity: While Krabi Town itself lacks beaches, it's conveniently close to some of Krabi's most beautiful shores, including Railay Beach, Ao Nang Beach, and the tranquil Klong Muang Beach, all easily accessible by bus, taxi, or boat.

Exploration Hub: The town is perfectly positioned as a launchpad for exploring Krabi's attractions and embarking on island-hopping adventures across Thailand's stunning Andaman Sea.

Essential Insights on Krabi Town

Krabi Town's charm lies in its non-typical tourist path character, preserving an authentic vibe. It serves as a crucial link between the mainland and the enchanting islands of the Andaman Sea, thanks to its proximity to the airport and ferry services. The town is a treasure trove of affordable dining, lively bars, and local markets, making it a favorite among individual travelers and backpackers who often extend their stay to soak in its idyllic ambiance.

Optimal Visit Times

The best period to visit Krabi and its surroundings is from November to April, with the peak travel months being January and February. The monsoon season from May to October sees a decline in visitors, offering a quieter but wetter experience.

Things to do in Krabi town

Krabi Town, with its picturesque setting by the Krabi River and a mix of natural wonders and cultural experiences, offers a unique blend of activities for travelers. From exploring ancient caves to tasting the local street food, here's a rundown of the top things to do in Krabi Town that promise an unforgettable stay.

1) Krabi River and the Iconic Crab Statue

What to Do: Take a leisurely stroll along the waterfront to admire the scenic river views and the famous crab statue symbolizing Krabi. The serene river ambience is perfect for relaxation and photography.

Must-Experience: Rent a long-tail boat to explore the mangrove forests leading to the mesmerizing Khao Khanab Nam Caves.

2) Wat Kaew Korawaram

Location: Situated atop a hill in the town center, this striking white temple is known for its elaborate staircase adorned with colorful snake sculptures.

Why Visit: It's free to enter and offers a peaceful retreat as well as insight into Buddhist practices and architecture.

3) Khao Khanap Nam Cave

Adventure Awaits: Accessible by a short and affordable longtail boat ride, this cave is a natural wonder set within the iconic limestone cliffs visible from the pier.

Highlights: Watch out for playful monkeys near the entrance and explore the cave's interior to see the fascinating, albeit not real, oversized skeletons displayed as part of the Krabi Biennial.

4) Mangrove Walkway

Discover Nature: A hidden gem in Krabi Town, this elevated walkway stretches 400 meters into the mangroves, offering a unique perspective on the local ecosystem, home to frogs, birds, crabs, and monitor lizards.

Location Tip: Start your mangrove adventure near the Grand Mansion Hotel on Uttaradit Road.

5) Krabi Town Night Market & Walking Street

Culinary Delights & Shopping: Krabi Town comes alive at night with its markets, where you can savor local cuisine, shop for souvenirs, and immerse yourself in the vibrant local culture.

Krabi Town Walking Street: Open Friday to Sunday evenings, this weekend market draws crowds for its street food, clothes, and handicrafts.

Fresh Food Market (Talad Sod): A daily market from 4 PM to 9 PM focusing on vegetables, fruits, and fantastic food stalls.

Chao Fah Night Market: This waterfront night market operates daily from 6 PM to midnight, offering a budget-friendly dining experience among locals and tourists alike.

Local Tip

Don't miss the delicious samosas at the stand on the edge of the Talad Sod Market. The friendly owners are known for their warm hospitality and love for football chats.

Why Krabi Town?

Krabi Town offers a rich tapestry of experiences that cater to nature lovers, culture enthusiasts, and foodies alike. Its laid-back atmosphere combined with the abundance of activities makes it a must-visit destination for those looking to explore beyond the typical tourist trails. Whether you're venturing through the mangrove forests, uncovering the secrets of ancient caves, or indulging in the local culinary scene, Krabi Town promises an array of unforgettable experiences.

Tiger Cave Temple Overview

Widely recognized as Krabi Town's premier landmark, the Tiger Cave Temple, or Wat Tham Sua, is an essential visit for anyone in the area. Situated on a limestone cliff approximately 280 meters above ground, visitors are challenged to ascend 1237 steps to reach the top. The effort is well rewarded with stunning views of the limestone formations that characterize Krabi's landscape.

Journey from Krabi Town to Railay Beach

For those stationed in Krabi Town, a trip to the internationally acclaimed Railay Beach, along with the neighboring Phra Nang Beach, is highly recommended. Renowned for their breathtaking limestone cliffs and crystal-clear turquoise waters, these beaches rank among Krabi's finest. Railay is a popular vacation spot, offering an array of excellent hotels and bungalows. A short 20-minute longtail boat ride from Krabi Town's waterfront can take you to this idyllic location for a memorable day trip.

Top Excursions from Krabi Town

Krabi Town's strategic position makes it a fantastic base for exploring the region's highlights. Options include visiting elephant sanctuaries, island hopping around Krabi's spectacular islets, and more. Tours can be arranged locally or booked online for convenience, with platforms like GetYourGuide offering well-reviewed experiences. Top tour recommendations include the Hong Islands, the 4 Island tour featuring Chicken Islands and Koh Poda, the Krabi Elephant Sanctuary, and the Emerald Pool.

Traveling from Ao Nang to Krabi Town

Visitors in Ao Nang should consider a day or half-day excursion to Krabi Town, perhaps to explore the famed night market. The most budget-friendly transport option is the Songthaew (red shared taxis), costing 50 baht per person for about a 30-minute journey. There's no set schedule, as Songthaews depart when full. For a more comfortable ride, air-conditioned taxis are available for around 300 Baht. Alternatively, renting a scooter offers the freedom to explore at one's pace.

Arriving in Krabi Town

Krabi's airport, situated roughly 13 kilometers from the town center, is accessible by direct flights from Bangkok. Upon arrival, visitors can choose between a taxi (approximately 800 baht) or a bus service (around 150 baht) to reach the town. The Klong Jilad Pier, located about 4 kilometers from Krabi Town, serves ferries to Phuket, Koh Phi Phi, Koh Lanta, and Koh Jum.

Accommodation Recommendations in Krabi Town

1. **Pak-Up Hostel:** A top-rated backpacker hostel located in the heart of town, known for its cleanliness and prime location.

2. **Hello House:** A charming, affordable guesthouse near the night market, offering simple yet clean accommodations.

3. **Family Tree Hotel:** A stylish boutique hotel in the town center, perfect for a comfortable stay.

4. **The Brown Hotel:** A chic 3-star hotel celebrated for its elegant decor and welcoming atmosphere.

Top Attractions in Krabi

Railay Beach

Railay Beach, located on the Railay Peninsula in Krabi, Thailand, stands as one of the country's most awe-inspiring destinations. Renowned for its dramatic limestone cliffs, crystal-clear turquoise waters, lush palm trees, and pristine sandy beaches, Railay offers a postcard-perfect tropical paradise. This destination is a hub for a variety of memorable activities and attractions, ranging from rock climbing and kayaking to snorkeling, hiking, and lounging on some of Thailand's finest beaches. Despite its popularity, Railay Beach retains its legendary charm, making it an essential stop on any Krabi itinerary.

Useful Insights for Your Railay Beach Adventure

For those seeking exceptional accommodation, the Hotel Rayavadee, with its expansive pool by the beach, comes highly recommended. Railay Peninsula is home to four of Krabi's most exquisite beaches: Railay Beach, Railay Beach East, the iconic Phra Nang Beach, and the secluded Tonsai Beach. It's important to note that access to Railay is exclusively by sea, with regular longtail boat services from Ao Nang Beach and Krabi Town. Additionally, Railay's magnificent limestone cliffs are a magnet for climbing enthusiasts, offering courses for all levels which can be booked through GetYourGuide.

Top Experiences at Railay Beach

Railay Beach is a treasure trove of activities and sights. With four stunning beaches, captivating attractions, and a plethora of excursions and activities, visitors are spoilt for choice. Here's a snapshot of the best experiences Railay has to offer:

Railay Beach: This iconic beach is a highlight of the peninsula, boasting emerald waters and towering rock formations that create an idyllic setting. The soft sand and absence of stones or corals make it perfect for swimming. Evenings on the beach are magical, with breathtaking sunsets and lively fire shows during peak season. Additionally, a selection of restaurants and bars offer the perfect spots for relaxation and enjoyment by the sea.

Tip: The Railay Village Resort, situated directly on the beach, impresses guests with its dual pools, exceptional location, and serene, well-maintained gardens.

Railay Beach encapsulates the essence of Krabi's natural beauty, offering a blend of relaxation and adventure that makes it a must-visit destination for travelers. Whether you're seeking the thrill of outdoor sports, the tranquility of a beachside retreat, or simply to immerse yourself in the breathtaking scenery, Railay delivers an unforgettable experience. Its unique combination of accessible yet secluded beaches, along with a variety of activities to suit all interests, ensures that every visit is filled with wonder and excitement.

Phi Phi Islands

The Phi Phi archipelago, a mesmerizing cluster of six islands, is a jewel in Thailand's Andaman Sea, located merely 40 km from Phuket. Among these, Phi Phi Don and Phi Phi Leh stand out as the most celebrated, drawing visitors with their immaculate beaches, azure waters, and vibrant nightlife. These islands offer an idyllic escape, embodying the quintessential tropical paradise.

In addition to Phi Phi Don and Phi Phi Leh, the archipelago includes the smaller isles of Bida Nok, Bida Nai, and Ko Mai Phai, commonly referred to as Bamboo Island. The Phi Phi Islands gained international fame following the release of the 2000 film "The Beach," filmed on the shores of Ko Phi Phi Leh. Another notable site on Ko Phi Phi Leh is the "Viking Cave," known for its lucrative edible bird's nest industry.

Characterized by their dramatic cliffs, lush jungles, pristine white sand beaches, and crystal-clear waters, the Phi Phi Islands present a breathtakingly beautiful landscape. Remarkably, the islands are devoid of roads, and most remain largely untouched by human development, preserving their natural beauty. This absence of urbanization makes the Phi Phi Islands among the world's remaining pristine environments.

Accessible from both Phuket and Krabi, the Phi Phi Islands are easily reached by a 45-minute speedboat ride or a 90-minute ferry journey. This convenience makes it possible for travelers to immerse themselves in the islands' untouched beauty and tranquil ambiance, whether for a day trip or an extended stay. The Phi Phi Islands invite you to experience their unspoiled splendor, promising an unforgettable adventure in one of Thailand's most iconic destinations.

Ao Nang Beach

Ao Nang Beach, the principal beachfront destination on Krabi's mainland, captivates visitors with its stunning shores and dramatic limestone cliffs setting the scene. Stretching over 2 kilometers, Ao Nang Beach is the vibrant heart of the area, fringed by a promenade bustling with bars, restaurants, and shops. Beyond its main beach, Ao

Nang boasts an array of exquisite beaches, regarded among Thailand's most picturesque, with velvety sands, azure waters, and palm trees nestled amongst majestic rocks, offering a breathtaking panorama. But what are the hidden gems and the most serene spots for an idyllic beach getaway in Ao Nang?

Centrally located, Ao Nang Beach serves as the focal point of the region, attracting the majority of its visitors. The beachside main street, along with its adjoining alleys, hosts a variety of shops, tour operators, massage parlors, eateries, and supermarkets, making it an ideal base for exploring Krabi's enchanting islands or discovering nearby dreamy shores. Additionally, Ao Nang is renowned for its spectacular sunsets, adding a magical touch to every holiday experience.

The beach's eastern end, known for its prominent cliffs, offers a more tranquil ambiance, making it perfect for those looking to swim and sunbathe away from the crowd. This area is devoid of longtail boats, providing a peaceful retreat.

Tip: Positioned directly on Ao Nang Beach, the Centara Ao Nang Beach Resort & Spa Krabi offers an exceptional stay with its prime beachfront location, inviting pool, and elegant rooms. A stay here not only promises direct access to the beach's beauty but also ensures a memorable experience with top-notch amenities and breathtaking views, making it a standout choice for visitors to Ao Nang.

Tiger Cave Temple

 The Tiger Cave Temple, locally known as Wat Tham Sua, stands as one of Krabi's most adventurous and spiritually significant destinations. Renowned for its challenging ascent of 1,237 steps, visitors are rewarded with breathtaking panoramic views of Krabi's iconic limestone cliffs and lush rainforests upon reaching the summit. Beyond the physical exertion, the temple complex, including the main "Tiger Cave" and its

surrounding "wonderland rainforest," offers a serene and profound cultural experience, making it a must-visit site in Krabi.

Key Insights

The most economical route to Tiger Cave Temple is by taking a Red Bus from Krabi Town. Alternatively, well-reviewed guided tours, which often include visits to the Emerald Pool, are available online via platforms like GetYourGuide.

The temple's name is derived from a legend, and while no tigers reside there today, visitors can still see a paw imprint in the cave.

For those seeking accommodation, the Family Tree in Krabi Town and Whalecome Aonang in Ao Nang are highly recommended for their convenience and comfort.

The Climb

The journey to the summit of the Tiger Cave Temple is an intense physical challenge, involving a steep climb up 1,237 steps. Some steps are notably high, making the ascent particularly strenuous. However, the climb offers several rest spots with stunning views, making the effort worthwhile. At the peak, the sight of Krabi's limestone cliffs and the rainforest, alongside a majestic golden Buddha and other statues, offers a tranquil and rewarding experience. Many choose to stay until evening to witness the spectacular sunset.

Practical Advice for Visitors:

❖ It's essential to bring sufficient water, as the climb is demanding.

❖ Feeding the monkeys is discouraged due to their unpredictability.

❖ Consider wearing appropriate footwear and bringing a change of clothes.

❖ For those descending after sunset, carrying headlamps is advisable.

❖ Visiting during the early morning or late afternoon is recommended to avoid the midday heat. Sunset visits are particularly stunning.

Entrance and Tours

Admission to Tiger Cave Temple is free, with a suggested voluntary donation of 40 Baht for entering the Tiger Cave itself. The temple is open daily and can be visited at any time, with some visitors even choosing to spend the night on the temple terrace under the stars.

Various transport options are available from Krabi Old Town, Ao Nang, and Klong Muang Beach, ranging from private taxis to scooters. Additionally, joining a guided tour can offer a comprehensive experience, combining visits to Tiger Cave Temple with other attractions like the Hot Springs and Emerald Pools.

Accommodation Near Tiger Cave Temple

Krabi Town: The Family Tree Hotel offers chic, stylish accommodation, while the Sleep Well Hostel is a budget-friendly option for backpackers.

Ao Nang: The Holiday Inn Resort provides a luxurious stay on Ao Nang's sandy beach, and TAN Hostel x Cafe is favored by backpackers for its cozy ambiance and delicious breakfast.

For a spiritually enriching and physically challenging experience amidst Krabi's natural beauty, the Tiger Cave Temple is an unparalleled destination, promising memories that will last a lifetime.

Emerald Pool

Also known as Sa Morakot, the Emerald Pool is a captivating natural pool with a fresh, turquoise hue, fed by streams descending from the surrounding hills. Situated in Thailand's Krabi province, it ranks as a top excursion destination. Encased within a mystical jungle, it unveils two crystal-clear bodies of water: the iconic Emerald Pool and the Blue Pool. A brief trek through the forest offers a glimpse into an untouched ecosystem, leaving visitors in awe of the rainforest's distinct atmosphere. Those inclined to take a dip should remember to bring swimwear, as the pool's inviting waters offer a refreshing respite in a picturesque environment. Visiting the Emerald Pool stands out as a memorable highlight in Krabi, promising an experience to cherish indefinitely.

This travel guide provides crucial insights into the Emerald Pool in Krabi, illustrating why it's a must-visit. Ideal starting points include Klong Muang Beach, Ao Nang Beach, and Krabi Town, accessible via taxi or through organized tours. Early morning visits are advisable for a serene experience, with the Emerald Pool's allure at its peak. For accommodation guidance in Krabi, our comprehensive guide outlines the best options.

The journey to the Emerald Pool is an enchanting nature adventure, leading through a well-marked trail that spans approximately 1.4 kilometers into the jungle. Along the way, visitors encounter pristine streams, small ponds, and a rich diversity of tropical flora. The trail culminates at Sa Kaew, the Crystal Pool, before reaching the Emerald Pool, where the water's turquoise gleam offers a stunning visual treat.

Upon arrival, guests can indulge in the cool waters, with the pool's depth ranging from 1–2 meters — an inviting proposition for swimmers. The pool's captivating setting is a magnet for photographers, while the slippery limestone terrain necessitates caution. Bathing shoes are recommended due to the slippery rocks. The pool's mesmerizing colors stem from its high limestone and mineral content.

Accessing the Emerald Pool

Individuals can organize their own transport to the Emerald Pools. A taxi round trip from Krabi Town to the national park typically costs around 2,500 Baht, suitable for sharing. The 60-kilometer journey takes about an hour. To avoid crowds, an early start is recommended, ideally around 7:00 am. For additional sightseeing, consider stopping by the Tiger Cave Temple.

Tours to Emerald Pool

Various travel agencies in Krabi Town, Ao Nang Beach, and Klong Muang Beach offer excursions to the Emerald Pool, with the option to book online for reputable experiences. Tours generally include hotel pickup, lunch, and visits to the hot springs and Tiger Cave Temple, though they may be shared with other tourists. A notable perk of booking through GetYourGuide is the flexibility to cancel without charge up to 24 hours in advance.

Opening Hours & Admission

The Emerald Pool welcomes visitors from 8:30 am to 4:30 pm, with the Blue Pool opening later, accessible from 10:00 am. Entry fees are 400 baht for adults and 200 baht for children, with year-round access to the Emerald Pool; note that the Blue Pool is closed from May to October.

Accommodation Near Emerald Pool

For those pondering where to stay, Krabi Town, the nearest to the Emerald Pool, serves as an excellent base for exploration. The Family Tree Hotel offers boutique lodging in the heart of the old town, while the Sleep Well Hostel is a top choice for budget-conscious travelers. Ao Nang, another prime location, boasts a wide array of accommodations, including the beachfront Holiday Inn Resort Krabi and the cozy TAN Hostel x Cafe, known for its welcoming atmosphere and tasty breakfast.

Krabi Hot Springs

Tucked away within Krabi's verdant jungle in Thailand, the Krabi Hot Springs stand as a natural wonder, offering visitors a unique outdoor spa experience. This destination is an exceptional choice for those seeking to explore the mainland's natural beauty amidst their island-hopping adventures to Phi Phi Island and beyond.

Situated in the Khlong Thom District in the southern part of Krabi, this geothermal area is home to several thermal springs, with the Krabi Hot Stream near the renowned Emerald Pool and Blue Pool in the Khao Phra Bang Khram Nature Reserve being the highlight.

Visitors can indulge in the warmth of a natural hot spring waterfall, which cascades into a natural pool, creating an effect akin to a mineral-rich jacuzzi, before the water merges with the cooler currents of a nearby river.

Reaching the Natural Hot Stream from Krabi

For those stationed in popular tourist locales within Krabi Province, such as Ao Nang or Railay Beach, the most straightforward approach to experiencing the hot springs is through booking the well-regarded full-day Emerald Pool tour available at getyourguide.com. This excursion is perfectly tailored for those looking to explore the inland attractions, as it encompasses visits to:

- ❖ Emerald Pool, Blue Pool, & Crystal Pool
- ❖ Krabi Hot Springs
- ❖ Tiger Cave Temple Climb

Such a tour not only simplifies the logistics of visiting these natural landmarks but also enriches the experience by combining the thermal bliss of the hot springs with the serene beauty of the pools and the spiritual upliftment of the Tiger Cave Temple, making for an unforgettable day trip.

Phra Nang Cave Beach

Phra Nang Cave Beach, nestled near Ao Nang, stands as a quintessential paradise in Thailand, often gracing the front pages of numerous travel guides with its breathtaking beauty. This idyllic beach is a stunning spectacle, featuring towering rocks, a sea of mesmerizing turquoise hues, and a lush jungle backdrop, making it an absolute must-visit. Adding to its allure is the intriguing Phra Nang Cave, also known as the Princess Cave, renowned for its unique fertility shrine adorned with myriad phallic symbols.

Situated on the Railay Peninsula, Phra Nang Beach is accessible from Ao Nang only by sea. The most convenient and scenic route to this secluded paradise is by taking a longtail boat from Ao Nang Beach. For those seeking tranquility, the best times to explore this beach are during the early morning or late afternoon, when it's at its most serene.

Tip: While there's an exclusive luxury resort directly on Phra Nang Beach, visitors looking for more affordable lodging options might consider the nearby Railay Beach, known for its range of accommodation choices catering to various budgets.

Outdoor Activities in Krabi

Rock Climbing

Krabi is a premier destination for climbing enthusiasts, thanks to its impressive limestone cliffs. Climbers of all skill levels find the region's varied routes appealing, especially the dramatic rock faces at the Railay Peninsula. Phra Nang Beach and the relaxed Tonsai Beach are hotspots for climbers. Beginners eager to tackle Krabi's limestone can find expert-led courses on platforms like GetYourGuide.

Kayaking

Kayaking is a fantastic way to explore Krabi's stunning coastline, secluded beaches, and lush mangrove forests. While kayaks are available for rent at most resorts, joining a guided tour enhances the experience, allowing access to otherwise unreachable spots. Check out GetYourGuide for kayaking tours that often combine other exciting activities like quad biking and island hopping.

Island Hopping Tours

Krabi serves as an ideal base for island hopping, offering access to a plethora of breathtaking islands such as Koh

Jum, Koh Lanta, Koh Kradan, Koh Mook, Koh Bulon, and Koh Lipe. The region's proximity to these islands makes boat tours a popular choice for exploring the Andaman Sea's dreamy landscapes.

Swimming

The Klong Thom Hot Springs, nestled in a jungle near the Khao Phra Bang Khram Nature Reserve, offer a unique swimming experience. The springs' warm saltwater, reaching temperatures of 40–47°C, is believed to possess healing properties. Visitors can enjoy a dip in the cascading waterfall's numerous shaded pools and mineral baths.

Sunbathing

Ao Nang, evolving from a backpacker's haven to a tourist paradise, is Krabi's most lively and westernized beach. Guests can engage in a variety of activities, from leisurely spa treatments and rock climbing to kayaking, scuba diving, and shopping, making it a perfect spot for sunbathing and relaxation.

Local Cuisine and Dining Options

1) Maharat Market

Maharat Market is renowned for its vibrant street seafood scene, where the fragrant Thai spices fill the air. As you meander through the market, the offerings of sticky rice and tropical fruits are plentiful, ensuring you're well-fed. Venture into Maharat Soi for an array of spicy Thai curries and delectable seafood starting from just THB 30. Additionally, the early birds can catch the Maharat Morning market from 3:00 AM to 10:00 AM, showcasing fresh produce.

Must Try: Fish cakes, Stingray curry, Pad Thai

Location: Soi 10 Maharat Road, across from City Hotel Krabi Town

Hours: 4:00 PM – 9:00 PM

Cost: THB 50 - THB 200 for two

2) Krabi Walking Street

Krabi Walking Street transforms the town with its weekend buzz, offering an authentic slice of local life through its array of food stalls, affordable household items, and live entertainment.

Must Try: Baan Toy, Coconut Ice-cream, Spring Rolls

Location: 7 Khongkha Rd, Tambon Pak Nam, Amphoe Mueang Krabi

Hours: Friday to Sunday, 6:00 PM – 10:00 PM

Cost: THB 100 - THB 300 for two

3) Chao Fah Pier Market

Chao Fah Pier Market is a must-visit for food enthusiasts, featuring a bustling night market atmosphere where local stalls offer Krabi's finest seafood among other delights.

Must Try: Seafood, Spicy Papaya Salad, Fried Noodles

Location: Chao Fah Pier on Kong Ka Road Krabi Town, Krabi Town

Hours: 5:00 PM - 12:30 AM

Cost: THB 100 - THB 300 for two

4) May and Mark House

May and Mark House is the go-to for a Western breakfast, serving up exceptional coffee, cheese omelets, and a variety of vegetarian and Mexican dishes, along with freshly baked bread.

Must Try: Mexican Enchiladas, Breakfast Combos

Location: 34 Maharaj Road Soi 10 Paknam Krabi, Krabi

Hours: 7:00 AM − 9:00 PM

Cost: THB 600 for two

5) Taj Palace

Taj Palace offers an upscale dining experience with a focus on authentic Indian flavors, blending them with Thai cuisine to create unique dishes.

Must Try: Kebabs, Prawn Tikka

Location: 440, Tambon Ao Nang, Amphoe Mueang Krabi, Krabi

Hours: 11:00 AM – 12 Midnight

Cost: THB 1200 for two

6) Temple Flower

Temple Flower specializes in vegetarian cuisine, offering plant-based takes on classic dishes with a mix of Thai and Indian spices.

Must Try: Spring rolls, Yellow Curry, Salads

Location: Ao Nang, Mueang Krabi District, Krabi

Hours: 11:00 AM – 11:00 PM

Cost: THB 300 for two

7) Maharaja Indian Restaurant

Maharaja Indian Restaurant is celebrated for its Indian cuisine, providing a memorable dining experience with both Indian and international dishes.

Must Try: Chicken Tikka Masala, Mutton Rogan Josh, Palak Paneer

Location: 197 1, Tambon Sala Dan, Amphoe Ko Lanta, Krabi

Hours: 9:00 AM – 10:30 PM

Cost: THB 350 - THB 500 for two

8) Tanta

Tanta is acclaimed for its outstanding Thai and international culinary offerings, presented in a comfortable, air-conditioned environment.

Must Try: Crab Fried Rice, Shrimp, Mint Salad

Location: 204, Mueang Krabi District, Krabi

Hours: 10:00 AM – 10:30 PM

Cost: THB 1000 for two

This guide showcases the rich and diverse dining options available in Krabi, from street markets to upscale restaurants, catering to all tastes and preferences.

Exploring Shopping in Krabi

Krabi offers a shopping experience that rivals even Bangkok's, thanks to its scenic ocean views and delectable street food. Whether it's expansive malls or beloved walking streets, Krabi has a variety of shopping destinations to explore:

Discover batiks, jewelry, and handicrafts at Klong Muang Plaza, Maharaj Market, Chao Fah Market, and Krabi Town Walking Street, the latter two being the largest night markets in Krabi.

Ao Nang Walking Street is a hub of activity, featuring everything from malls and banks to nightclubs and seafood stalls.

For unique finds, visit Chock Dee Handmade Jewelry Shop, Krabi Souvenir Shop, and Sabai Ba Bars and Souvenirs.

Krabi's shopping malls, such as Vogue Department Store, Big C Mall, Outlet Village, and Victoria Fashion House, offer a mix of shopping, dining, and entertainment options.

Markets in Krabi

1) Krabi Town Walking Street (Krabi Night Market)

Open every weekend, this bustling market centered around a stage in Soi Maharaj is perfect for shopping, eating, and enjoying live performances. Offering a wide range of products, from fashion to household tools, and showcasing local artisans' work, it's an ideal spot for souvenir hunting. Bargaining is part of the experience, ensuring you get the best deals.

Address: Soi Maharaj 8, behind Vogue Department Store(VDS)

Timings: 5 PM to 10 PM, Friday to Sunday

2) Ao Nang's Catalunya Walking Street

Since its opening in 2007, this L-shaped marketplace has become a go-to for Krabi shopping, accessible via multiple entrances and filled with souvenir stalls. Dining options like the Tex-Mex restaurant and the Blue Orchid offer delicious meals and live music.

Address: Southern corner of Ao Nang Beach Road

Timings: 10 AM to 10 PM, daily

3) Maharaj Market

Known for its fresh local produce, the Maharaj market is the place for groceries or unique Thai spices. It's an enclosed market bustling with a variety of fresh goods and food stalls.

Address: Soi 7 off Mahajan Road in downtown Krabi, Krabi

Timings: 6 AM to 12 PM, daily

4) Chao Fah Market

As Krabi's largest night market, Chao Fah Market offers a lively dining scene with a variety of local and international cuisines. It's a bustling spot where food lovers can indulge in authentic flavors.

Address: Chao Fah Pier on Kong Ka Road Krabi Town, Krabi Town

Timings: 5 PM to Midnight, daily

Shopping Malls and Plazas in Krabi

1) Vogue Department Store

A three-story building in Krabi's center, offering branded goods, a gaming room, and karaoke, along with popular eateries, making it a perfect stop for a shopping spree.

Address: 76/1 Maharaj Road, Tambon Pak Nam, Amphoe Mueang Krabi, Krabi

Timings: 10 AM to 9 PM (Mon-Thurs) and 10:30 AM to 9:30 PM (Fri-Sun)

2) Klong Muang Plaza

A quaint mix of antique shops, beauty parlors, and eateries, offering a calm shopping experience with additional relaxation options like massage parlors.

Address: Nong Thale, Mueang Krabi District, Krabi

Timings: 3 PM to 7 PM (Sun and Tue)

3) Big C Mall

Known for its wide product range and lower prices on branded items, Big C Mall is a convenient one-stop for various shopping needs, from electronics to food.

Address: 34911 Phet Kasem Rd, Tambon Krabi Noi, Amphoe Mueang Krabi, Krabi

Timings: 8 AM to 10 PM, daily

4) Outlet Village Krabi

Offering significant discounts on branded items, the Outlet Village is a must-visit for bargain hunters, with tax refund options for non-residents.

Address: Moo 11 888 Phet Kasem Rd, Tambon Krabi Noi, Amphoe Mueang Krabi, Krabi

Timings: 10 AM to 8 PM, daily

Stores in Krabi for Unique Finds and Souvenirs

Krabi is not just about its breathtaking beaches and outdoor adventures; it's also a treasure trove for shoppers looking to bring back a piece of their holiday. Here are some unique stores in Krabi where you can find everything from handmade jewelry to custom suits and eclectic souvenirs:

1) Sabai Ba Bars and Souvenirs

Located near Tubkaak, Sabai Ba offers a unique combination of a restaurant, bar, and souvenir shop. It stands out for its use of recycled materials and fabrics. The ambiance is reminiscent of Arabian Nights, with Thai cushions, small tables, and colorful draperies. The menu offers a mix of Thai and International delicacies, with prices ranging from spring rolls at 120 bahts to seafood spaghetti at 220 bahts. The souvenir section features Thai-style handicrafts made from wood and ceramic, making it a perfect spot to pick up something special.

Location: 3P5X+F9 Nong Thale, Mueang Krabi District, Krabi, Thailand

Timings: 10 AM to 10 PM (Daily)

2) Chock Dee Handmade Jewelry Shop

Chock Dee is a haven for jewelry enthusiasts in Krabi. Known for its exceptional service and the artistry of its pieces, the shop offers a wide range of unique jewelry. Each piece is crafted with precision, making it an ideal place to find a special gift for your loved ones or a memorable keepsake for yourself.

Location: 142/6 Moo 2 Tambon Ao Nang, Amphoe Mueang Krabi, Chang Wat Krabi

Timings: 10 AM to 6 PM (Daily)

3) Victoria Fashion House

Gaining popularity for its handmade goods and professional-quality items, Victoria Fashion House is a must-visit for those looking to bring back custom-made clothing from Krabi. The store prides itself on the quality of its materials and the craftsmanship of its tailors. Customers can have custom suits made, with the process taking as little as three days for completion. It's an excellent choice for personalized shopping in Krabi, offering a touch of elegance to your wardrobe.

Location: 6024, Tambon Nong Thale, Amphoe Mueang Krabi, Krabi

Timings: 10 AM to 10 PM (Daily)

Each of these stores offers something unique to Krabi's shopping scene, from eco-friendly souvenirs and exquisite jewelry to bespoke tailoring services. They reflect the diverse and rich culture of Thailand, making them perfect stops for those looking to take a piece of Krabi home with them.

Exploring Nightlife in Krabi

Krabi's nightlife scene, with its relaxed vibe and diverse offerings, ensures that every visitor finds something to enjoy as the sun sets. Whether you're into serene beach lounges, vibrant markets, or thrilling performances, Krabi has it all. Here's a closer look at what you can expect when exploring nightlife and entertainment in Krabi:

1)Ao Nang Beach: The Nightlife Hub

Beachfront Lounges and Bars: Ao Nang transforms at night, with its beachfront dotted with lounges and bars. It's the perfect place to relax with a cocktail while enjoying live music and the sea breeze.

Variety of Dining Options: From local Thai dishes to international cuisine, the dining scene in Ao Nang caters to all taste buds, often with the added bonus of stunning sea views.

2) Krabi Town: A Lively Atmosphere

Local Markets: The night markets in Krabi Town are not just about shopping; they're a cultural experience. Sample the delicious street food, browse through souvenirs, and soak in the local vibe.

Bars and Clubs: While quieter than Ao Nang, Krabi Town still boasts a selection of bars and clubs for those looking to enjoy a drink and perhaps some dancing.

Unique Entertainment

Fire Shows: Especially popular in Railay Beach and Ao Nang, fire shows are a must-see. Watch in awe as skilled performers dance and juggle with fire, lighting up the night.

Cultural Shows: For a touch of Thai tradition, seek out venues that offer cultural shows, featuring graceful Thai dances and music.

3) Night Markets: A Feast for the Senses

Krabi Town Weekend Night Market: A highlight of Krabi's nightlife, this market is a paradise for food lovers and bargain hunters alike. From savory snacks to sweet treats, the culinary offerings are endless.

Islands and Beaches: Beyond Mainland Krabi

Railay Beach, Koh Phi Phi, and Koh Lanta: These nearby destinations also offer their unique nightlife experiences, from laid-back beach bars to lively clubs and bars.

Top Nightlife Destinations in Krabi

1) Boogie Bar, Ao Nang

Just steps away from the beach on Ao Nang Walking Street, Boogie Bar stands out with its seventies retro design, divided by the street itself. One side of the bar boasts seating, a pool table, and the main bar area, while the other side is home to a stage for regular cover band performances. These bands bring classic pop-rock hits to life, making Boogie Bar a must-visit for a fun night out. The bar serves a selection of popular drinks, including beer, cocktails, and soft drinks, ensuring a memorable evening in Krabi.

Location: Ao Nang, Mueang Krabi District, Krabi 81000

2) Bamboo Bar

Situated behind Railay Walking Street, Bamboo Bar offers a beachy vibe by day and turns into a vibrant party spot by night. Known for its excellent cocktails and live music, it's a prime location for enjoyment in Railay.

Location: Ao Nang, Krabi 81180, Thailand

3) Tew Lay Bar

Situated on Railay Beach's eastern side, Tew Lay Bar provides a serene setting for a night out with its rustic bamboo structure and relaxing melodies. A short walk along the beach's eastern track leads you to this gem, where you can admire the Andaman Sea, mangroves, and Krabi hills while enjoying cocktails and hammocks. Offering both Thai and International cuisine, it's one of Railay's original bars, perfect for a secluded evening.

Address: Railay Beach East Ao Nang, Krabi, Thailand

3) Ole Bar

Previously known as Old West Bar, Ole Bar is renowned for its friendly atmosphere, excellent music, and service. It's an ideal spot for an enjoyable evening with friends, offering board games, cocktails, and pool. Drinks are reasonably priced, making it a standout choice for a night out in Krabi Town.

Address: 91 Utarakit road, 83000 Krabi Town, Thailand

4) Last Bar

Although it no longer holds its title as the final bar on Railay's strip due to the area's expansion, Last Bar continues to be a popular choice for nightlife. With its beachside setting, affordable drink buckets, fire shows, and Muay Thai events, it promises an exciting evening. Despite the occasional long boxing match, the vibrant atmosphere keeps the crowd cheering.

Address: Railay Beach, Krabi, Thailand

5) Reggae Town Bar and Restaurant

Offering a rustic setting with wooden decor and a laid-back vibe near Patong Beach, Reggae Town Bar and Restaurant is a hub for reggae music fans. With live music nearly every day, a wide selection of drinks, and tasty snacks, it's a top pick for those looking to relax and enjoy the nightlife on Patong walking street.

Address: 48 Ao Nang, Mueang Krabi District, 81000 Krabi, Thailand

7-Day Itinerary in Krabi

Coastal Splendor and Evening Glow

Morning

Kickstart your journey in Krabi with a delightful breakfast at Chalita Cafe & Restaurant, where you can taste the local delicacies. Following breakfast, enjoy a leisurely exploration of Ao Nang Beach's pristine sands and immerse yourself in its tropical atmosphere.

Afternoon

Savor the fresh catch of the day at Krua Thara Seafood for lunch. After your meal, set off on a Krabi 4 Islands Snorkeling Tour by Longtail Boat. This adventure will allow you to discover the area's rich marine life and awe-inspiring karst landscapes.

Evening

As the evening sky paints itself with colors, relish a BBQ dinner during the Krabi 4 Islands Sunset Longtail Boat Tour, all while being surrounded by dramatic limestone cliffs. Conclude your day with a tranquil walk on Tup

Island (Koh Tup), which connects to the famous Chicken Island via a sandbar.

Exploring Ao Nang Beach

Nestled on the outskirts of Ao Nang, Krabi's bustling tourist center, Ao Nang Beach is a haven of fine sand and crystal-clear waters. With stunning vistas and a lively selection of bars and restaurants, it's the perfect place for sunbathing or swimming in the Andaman Sea.

Krabi 4 Islands Snorkeling Adventure

Embark on a day-long journey by longtail boat to explore four iconic islands: Poda Island, Tup Island, Chicken Island, and Railay Beach. This tour offers ample opportunities for snorkeling, swimming, photography, and relaxation on the idyllic beaches.

Available for booking at getyourguide.com, starting at $29.60 per person.

Day 2: Cultural Gems and Culinary Delights

Morning

Begin your day with a visit to the revered Tiger Cave Temple (Wat Tham Suea). Explore the temple grounds and then have a hearty breakfast at May & Mark's House.

Afternoon

After lunch, participate in a traditional Krabi Cooking Class at Thai Charm Cooking School with Meal. You'll learn how to cook authentic Thai dishes, including a trip to the local market for fresh ingredients.

Evening

Enjoy dinner at Ruen Mai Restaurant, renowned for its refined ambiance and exquisite Thai cuisine. Cap off the evening with a gentle walk on Phra Nang Beach (Phranang Beach), known for its extraordinary cave and rock formations.

Explore Krabi's Sunset and Islands

Experience a romantic sunset with a BBQ dinner on the beach. Visit Yawasom Island, a great spot for snorkeling, as well as Poda Island, Chicken Island, Tup, and Mor Island. Book at getyourguide.com starting from $41.89 per person.

Discover Tup Island

Tiny Tup Island, situated merely 500 feet from Mor Island, offers a stunning sandbar walk between the islets during low tide, surrounded by turquoise waters. Visit Viator.com for more details.

Cultural and Culinary Exploration

Tiger Cave Temple (Wat Tham Suea): A spiritual haven known for its 1,237 steps leading to a magnificent Buddha statue, offering panoramic views of Krabi and the Andaman Sea. Admission is free.

Thai Charm Cooking School: Master the art of Thai cuisine in a hands-on cooking class, where you'll choose 7 dishes to prepare and enjoy. Prices start from $46.08 per person.

Phra Nang Beach (Phranang Beach): This beach is famous for its golden sands, limestone cliffs, and the unique Phra

Nang Cave, offering a chance to see bioluminescent plankton under the right conditions.

Day 3: Island Splendors and Culinary Joy

Morning

Begin your day at Lae Lay Grill, where breakfast comes with breathtaking views of the Andaman Sea. After breakfast, embark on the Krabi Hong Islands Day Tour by Longtail Boat, exploring some of the most picturesque islands in the area.

Afternoon

After enjoying a tasty lunch at Chalita Cafe & Restaurant once more, continue your island adventure with the Krabi Hong Islands Boat Tour, which includes a visit to the Panorama Viewpoint for stunning views.

Evening

Dine at Wang Sai Seafood in the evening to enjoy a relaxed atmosphere and delicious meals. End your day with a peaceful visit to Khlong Nam Sai Lagoon, where you can kayak through crystal clear freshwater and, if you're feeling adventurous, opt for an ATV ride.

Explore Krabi's Natural Beauty

Hong Islands Day Tour by Longtail Boat: A journey to the Hong Islands offers snorkeling in the vibrant waters of the Andaman Sea, a delicious lunch, and valuable insights from knowledgeable guides. Available from $34.91 per person at Getyourguide.com.

Khlong Nam Sai Lagoon with Kayaking & Optional ATV: Discover the secluded beauty of Khlong Nam Sai, a crystal-clear freshwater lagoon, by kayak. For added excitement, choose the ATV option. This experience starts from $34 per person at Getyourguide.com.

Hong Islands Boat Tour with Panorama Viewpoint: This tour takes you through the enchanting waters of the Hong Islands, including a visit to a magical oasis of mangrove forests and crystal-clear waters. Ascend to the viewpoint for breathtaking views of the landscapes and waters. Priced from $38.54 per person at Getyourguide.com.

Day 4: Adventure, Caves, and Emerald Pools

Morning

Start your adventurous day with a hearty breakfast at Carnivore Steak and Grill. Then, get ready for an exciting Sea Kayaking experience in Ao Thalane, with an optional full-day excursion to Hong Island. This activity offers a unique way to explore Krabi's stunning coastal mangroves and hidden caves.

Sea Kayaking in Ao Thalane & Optional Full-Day Hong Island: From $33.51 per person at getyourguide.com.

Afternoon

For lunch, visit the secluded Emerald Cave (Tham Morakot), known for its hidden beach accessed through a thrilling cave entrance. After lunch, relax and soak in the natural beauty of the Emerald Pool (Sa Morakot), a stunning natural pool in the midst of lush rainforest.

Emerald Cave (Tham Morakot): Explore this unique attraction in the Trang islands, famous for its vivid green waters. Booking available at viator.com.

Emerald Pool (Sa Morakot): Dive into the crystal-clear, blue-green waters of this natural pool, surrounded by dense forest and serene nature.

Evening

Enjoy a peaceful dinner at Ruen Mai Restaurant, offering exquisite Thai cuisine in a delightful setting. Wrap up your day with a visit to the Trickeye Museum for fun and interactive optical illusion art, perfect for capturing memorable photos of your trip.

Trickeye Museum: Open daily from 10 am until 7 pm, with last admissions at 6 pm. Located at 130 1 Phangnga Road, Tambon Talat, Mueang Phuket, Phuket, 83000

Day 5: Krabi - Relaxation, Rejuvenation, and Rock Formations

Morning

Begin your day with a serene breakfast at Lae Lay Grill, where you can relish the refreshing ocean breeze. After breakfast, embark on a private long-tail boat excursion to the tranquil Krabi Private Long Tail Boat to the 4 Islands. Here, you'll have the opportunity to unwind on secluded beaches and explore hidden coves, immersing yourself in the natural beauty of Krabi's coastal gems.

Private Long Tail Boat to the 4 Islands: Enjoy a private, half-day island hopping tour on a traditional long-tail boat, visiting the renowned 4 Islands of Krabi. From $259.71 per group up to 2 people at Getyourguide.com.

Afternoon

Return to Ao Nang for a delightful lunch at Krua Thara Seafood, followed by a leisurely afternoon at the Mu Ko Lanta National Park (Mu Koh Lanta National Marine Park). Discover the park's diverse marine life and pristine beaches, soaking in the tranquility of this natural haven.

Mu Ko Lanta National Park (Mu Koh Lanta National Marine Park): Explore the park's well-maintained diving spots and stunning landscapes. Located in Kho Lanta, Krabi, 81150. Open daily.

Evening

Indulge in a cozy, homely dinner experience at May & Mark's House, where you can savor authentic Thai dishes in a welcoming atmosphere. Conclude your day with a visit to Railay Beach, accessible only by boat and renowned for its breathtaking limestone cliffs and crystal-clear waters.

Railay Beach: Explore the interconnected beaches of Railay, including Tonsai, Phra Nang, East Railay, and West Railay, each offering picturesque white sand beaches and a tranquil ambiance perfect for relaxation and exploration.

Day 6: Krabi - Scenic Views, Shopping, and Spectacular Sunset

Morning

Begin your day with a refreshing breakfast at Wang Sai Seafood, enjoying the gentle morning sea breeze. After breakfast, embark on an excursion to the nearby Poda Island (Koh Poda) and Chicken Island (Koh Gai), where you can indulge in some snorkeling and relax on the pristine beaches.

Poda Island (Koh Poda) Tours and Tickets: Experience the pristine beauty of Poda Island, known for its dramatic limestone formations, white sandy beaches, and excellent snorkeling opportunities off the nearby coral reef. Located in Krabi, 81000. Book at Viator.com.

Afternoon

After returning to Ao Nang for a delightful lunch at May & Mark's House, make your way to Phuket Old Town. Spend the afternoon exploring the charming historical streets, vibrant local markets, and the architectural delights that the town has to offer.

Phuket Old Town Tours and Tickets: Discover the often-overlooked treasures of Phuket Old Town, with its 19th-century architectural delights, temples, museums, and restaurants, offering a rich cultural experience and fantastic photo opportunities. Located in Phuket, 83000. Book at Viator.com.

Evening

For dinner, treat yourself to a sophisticated dining experience at Lae Lay Grill, offering a cliffside view and a wide selection of fresh seafood. Conclude your day with the Krabi 7 Islands Sunset by Grande Longtail Boat with BBQ, witnessing a breathtaking sunset that serves as a perfect farewell to the Andaman Sea.

Krabi 7 Islands Sunset by Grande Longtail Boat with BBQ: Enjoy a scenic sunset tour of the 7 Islands, complete with a BBQ dinner. This tour promises a memorable evening with stunning views, delicious food, and the serene beauty of the Andaman Sea at dusk.

Sunset and BBQ on the 7 Islands via Grande Longtail Boat

Embark on a scenic boat journey from Krabi across the Andaman Sea, set against the breathtaking scenery of seven exquisite islands. Experience the vivid hues of a sunset and savor a delicious BBQ dinner.

Starting at $75.12 per person

Available at Getyourguide.com

Morning

Start your last day in Krabi with a leisurely breakfast at Ruen Mai Restaurant, enjoying the serene ambiance. Proceed to embark on the Krabi to Khao Sok Cheow Lan Lake Day Trip, immersing yourself in the majestic limestone cliffs and the vibrant green hues of the lake's waters.

Afternoon

Enjoy a hearty lunch at Carnivore Steak and Grill, savoring their specialty dishes. Spend your afternoon in the heart of nature at Khao Sok National Park, venturing through ancient rainforests, spotting exotic wildlife, and enjoying a peaceful river cruise.

Evening

Cap off your week-long journey with a memorable farewell dinner at Ruen Mai Restaurant, reflecting on the unforgettable moments and culinary delights experienced in Krabi.

Experience the enchanting beauty of Cheow Lan Lake within Khao Sok National Park on a comprehensive day tour from Krabi. Engage in activities like kayaking, swimming, and a secret cave hike, complemented by a delightful Thai lunch at a floating restaurant.

Starting from $125.67 per person

Available at Getyourguide.com

Krabi Travel Budget and Tips

Daily Budget in Krabi

For meals, snacks, and drinks per person: Around €50 ($55) if opting for Western cuisine, and about €25 ($27) for Thai cuisine, excluding accommodation and flights.

Currency and Banking Insights

It's wise to exchange some currency to Thai Baht before arriving. The Baht offers good value, especially for USD, GBP, or EUR holders.

Thailand favors cash transactions, and card payments may incur a 3% extra fee. While ATMs are available, they charge a fee of 220 Baht (€6 or $7) per transaction, except for AEON ATMs which charge 150 Baht (€4 or $5). To save, withdraw larger amounts less frequently and use AEON ATMs when possible.

Acquiring a SIM Card in Thailand

To avoid roaming fees, purchase a tourist SIM card. Avoid airport vendors for better rates. Options include a 15-day unlimited data SIM for 699 Baht (under €18 or $20) or an 8-day plan for 499 Baht (under €11 or $12). Bring identification for registration.

Consider an e-SIM for convenience, albeit at a higher cost, with options for heavy or light data users.

Health and Hygiene Practices

Drinking tap water is not recommended. Opt for boiled or treated water. To minimize plastic waste, refill bottles at establishments offering safe drinking water.

Transportation in Krabi

Krabi is navigable on foot within town limits. For longer distances, public buses, taxis, and tuk-tuks are available.

Renting a scooter offers freedom and adventure, requiring only your passport and a valid driving license, without a cash deposit.

Optimal Time for Visiting Krabi

The best travel period is from November to April, avoiding the monsoon season. This is peak season due to favorable weather, making some attractions and activities more accessible but also more costly.

Getting to and Around Krabi

Budget Flights: To save on travel costs, consider budget airlines for your trip to Krabi.

Visit Krabi in the Sunshine Season

The ideal period for a Krabi visit is from November to May, promising sunny weather and serene seas. Avoid September and October, the peak rainy season.

Pack Light and Smart for the Beach

With Krabi's typically hot and humid climate, opt for light and airy clothes. Essential items include swimwear, sandals, sunblock, shades, and possibly mosquito spray.

Bring a Universal Adaptor

Thailand uses Type A, B, and C electrical sockets. A universal adaptor simplifies things.

Currency and Cash Access is Easy

In Krabi, especially in tourist hubs like Ao Nang, you'll find ample ATMs, banks, and currency exchange services. Notable banks include ANZ, CIMB, OCBC, UOB, and Standard Chartered.

Krabi's Got You Covered

Krabi is very accommodating to travelers; your passport and cash are the essentials. Anything else can be found in local stores, minimarts, or pharmacies.

Learn a Bit of Thai

While Thai is the primary language, some English is spoken in tourist areas. Knowing basic Thai phrases, like "Sawa dee" (hello) and "Khob khun krab/ka" (thank you), is beneficial.

Exploring Beyond Krabi

Island day trips, also known as island hopping, rank among the top attractions in Krabi. However, it's important to acknowledge that these trips tend to draw large crowds, particularly during peak seasons.

To circumvent the crowds, the best strategy is to embark early in the day and consider booking a private tour. While chartering a private boat can be prohibitively expensive in many destinations, Thailand offers a more accessible option.

For groups of four or more travelers, you can charter your own boat for less than €50 ($55) per person. Here are some available options:

Private Luxury Long Tail Boat Island Hopping Tour from Krabi: Experience the beauty of the islands in comfort and privacy.

Private Island-Hopping Tour from Ao Nang or Krabi: Enjoy the exclusivity of a luxury long tail boat excursion departing from either Ao Nang or Krabi.

To book your private island-hopping experience, visit getyourguide.com and select the option that best suits your travel plans. This approach not only provides a more intimate and customizable experience but also allows you to explore the islands at your own pace, away from the bustling crowds.

Safety and Health Factors

Safety and Security: Although Thailand is generally a peaceful country, political unrest can escalate quickly, transforming it into a tense situation. Public demonstrations, though rare, can unexpectedly disrupt travel plans. Avoid areas known for demonstrations, and try not to get involved if you find yourself near one. Thailand experiences a high crime rate, including physical assaults on foreign visitors. There have been instances of tourists being ambushed. Additionally, Thailand has locations known for sexual assaults. Exercise caution in hotels and on the streets. Given the history of drink spiking, be wary of accepting drinks from strangers. If possible, avoid late nights at bars. Street crimes, including robbery by thieves and pickpockets on secluded roads, are also a concern. Avoid isolated areas and do not venture out alone at night. Keep a close eye on your credit and debit cards, and other important documents, as fraud is common. Avoid excessive drinking to maintain your awareness.

Driving in Thailand is permissible with an international driver's license. Road accidents, often fatal, are a concern, especially at night. Always don't forget to wear a helmet when riding a motorcycle. While there are many exciting activities in Thailand, always exercise caution.

Regional Laws and Practices

Local laws and customs in Thailand are strict, and arrest can lead to severe consequences. Do not transport or distribute narcotics. Never make derogatory comments about the Thai monarchy, as this can lead to long prison sentences. Always carry your passport, as failure to do so can lead to arrest by the authorities.

Health

While not universally available, Thailand has numerous excellent private hospitals equipped with advanced technology. Carry insect repellent, as dengue fever is common. Consult your doctor about necessary vaccines 6 to 8 weeks before your trip to ensure you are properly immunized. For emergency medical assistance, dial 1669.

Natural Disasters

The monsoon season, starting in May and lasting until October, brings heavy rains that can cause flooding and fatalities in some areas of Thailand. Earthquakes are rare but can be devastating when they occur.

Money

ATMs are widely available. The official currency is the Thai Baht; other currencies can be exchanged, except for US dollars, euros, Scottish, and Irish banknotes.

Tipping in Thailand

In-restaurant gratuity: $1.

Tip amount at hotel: $1.

Tipping in a cab: $1.

FAQs

What vaccinations are recommended before travelling to Krabi?

Before traveling to Thailand, consider vaccinations for Hepatitis A, Typhoid, Hepatitis B, Japanese Encephalitis, Malaria, Rabies, and Yellow Fever.

Should I be concerned about insects in Krabi?

Yes, insects like mosquitoes, ticks, and fleas can spread diseases, many of which cannot be prevented with vaccines or medicine. Taking steps to prevent bug bites is advisable.

How can I prevent bug bites?

- Wear long-sleeved shirts, long pants, and hats to cover exposed skin.
- Use an appropriate insect repellent.
- Treat clothing and gear with permethrin and avoid using permethrin directly on the skin.

- ❖ Prefer staying and sleeping in air-conditioned or screened rooms.
- ❖ Use a bed net if sleeping areas are exposed to the outdoors.

Should I worry about germs in Krabi?

To avoid getting sick or spreading illnesses:

- ❖ Wash your hands often, especially before eating.
- ❖ Use hand-sanitizer containing at least 60% alcohol when water and soap aren't available.
- ❖ Avoid touching your face with unwashed hands.
- ❖ When sneezing or coughing, make sure to use your sleeve or a tissue to cover your mouth and nose.
- ❖ Avoid close contact with sick individuals.
- ❖ Stay in your accommodation if you are sick, except to get medical care.

What diseases and threats are present in Thailand?

You may encounter diseases such as Hepatitis A, Typhoid, Hepatitis B, Japanese Encephalitis, Malaria, Rabies, and Yellow Fever.

Should I be cautious of animals in Thailand?

Yes, avoid close contact with animals as they can transmit diseases like rabies. Be especially cautious around bats, monkeys, dogs, sea animals (including jellyfish), and snakes. Consider purchasing medical evacuation insurance for emergencies.

Should I be careful about what I eat and drink in Thailand?

Yes, to reduce the risk of illness from unclean food and water, follow these guidelines:

Eat:

- ❖ Food that is cooked and served hot
- ❖ Hard-cooked eggs
- ❖ Fruits and vegetables you have peeled yourself or washed in clean water
- ❖ Pasteurized dairy products

Avoid eating

- ❖ Food served at room temperature
- ❖ Street food
- ❖ Raw or soft-cooked eggs
- ❖ Raw or undercooked meat or fish

- ❖ Unwashed or unpeeled raw fruits and vegetables
- ❖ Unpasteurized dairy products

Drink

- ❖ Sealed bottled water
- ❖ Disinfected water
- ❖ Ice made with bottled or disinfected water
- ❖ Carbonated drinks
- ❖ Hot coffee or tea
- ❖ Pasteurized milk

Avoid drinking

- ❖ Tap or well water
- ❖ Ice made with tap or well water
- ❖ Drinks made with tap or well water
- ❖ Unpasteurized milk

Safety in Krabi

General Safety: Krabi is considered moderately safe for travelers. The crime level has decreased in recent years, making it relatively safe for tourists.

Walking in Krabi: The risk of being attacked is very low, making Krabi safe for walking, even at night.

Solo Female Travelers: Krabi is generally safe for women traveling alone, with minimal risks related to gender-based violence.

Climate and Weather

Rainy Season: The highest chances of rain are in September, October, and November.

Warmest Months: The hottest months are March and April, with temperatures reaching up to 35°C (95°F). February and May also see high temperatures.

Summer Weather: Expect temperatures up to 35°C (95°F) during the day. The summer season includes February through September, with relatively high temperatures and a mix of sunny and rainy days.

Winter Weather: Krabi does not experience a typical winter. December, considered winter, maintains warm temperatures around 31°C (87°F), with no snow.

Weather in May: Expect daytime temperatures around 34°C (93°F) and nighttime temperatures around 24°C (7°F), with a 57% chance of rain.

Traffic: Traffic congestion can be a problem in Krabi, with residents expressing dissatisfaction with traffic conditions.

Public Transport: Krabi does not have a subway system. Transportation options include buses, taxis, and rental vehicles.

Pollution: Krabi is fairly clean, with low levels of pollution, making it a pleasant destination for those concerned about environmental quality.

Green Spaces: There are parks and gardens in Krabi, offering green spaces for relaxation and enjoyment.

Tourist Satisfaction: Tourists generally rate their stay in Krabi favorably, appreciating its cleanliness and upkeep.

Health Care Quality: Both public and private healthcare facilities in Krabi are of high quality, providing reliable medical care to travelers.

Emergency Medical Care Cost: Travelers should be prepared for the high cost of emergency medical care in Krabi. Securing comprehensive travel insurance that includes coverage for medical costs is recommended.

Language and Useful Phrases

UNDERSTANDING THE BASICS OF THAI LANGUAGE

The Thai language is renowned for its complexity. Its script, which may appear as intricate doodles to the uninitiated, especially after a festive evening, and its tonal nature, make it a daunting language to master.

Unlike languages such as Spanish, Thai does not feature gendered nouns, tenses, or plural forms. However, the structure of sentences can vary depending on the speaker's gender.

Chan / Phom

Take, for instance, the pronouns Chan and Phom, both translating to 'I' in English. The choice between them is gender-specific.

To express apologies in Thai:

* ❖ Male speakers would say – Phom kor toht (krab)
* ❖ Female speakers would say – Chan kor toht (kha)
* ❖ The addition of (krab/kha) is also gender-specific, marking politeness at the end of sentences or phrases.

Krab / Kha

These terms, Krab for males and Kha for females, are appended to sentences to denote politeness. Consequently, the widely used greeting "Sawadee" transforms into "Sawadee kha" when uttered by a woman and "Sawadee krab" when said by a man.

BASIC PHRASES IN THAI

Here are essential Thai phrases that will greatly enhance your interaction with locals, demonstrating your respect and appreciation for their culture. Remembering the basics like "Hello" – sawadee (krab/kha) and "Thank you" – Kop kun (krab/kha) will significantly enrich your experience in Thailand.

- ❖ Hello – Sawadee (krab/kha)
- ❖ Goodbye – Lakon (krab/kha)
- ❖ Please – Dai broht
- ❖ Thank You – Kop kun (krab/kha)
- ❖ You're welcome – Duay kwaam yin dee (krab/kha)
- ❖ Excuse me – Kor a nu yaart (krab/kha)
- ❖ I'm sorry – Chan/Phom kor toht (krab/kha)

- Do you speak English? – Khun poot paa saa ang grit daai mai? (krab/kha)
- I don't understand – Chan/Phom mai kaow jai (krab/kha)
- Where is the bathroom? – Hong naam you tee nai? (krab/kha)
- How much does this cost? – Raa kar tao rai? (krab/kha)
- Enjoy your meal – Ta~n hai a roi (krab/kha)
- What is the Wi-Fi password? – Ra hat pa~n Wi Fi lek a rai? (krab/kha)
- Could you take a photo of us, please? – Khun chuuay taai roop puuak rao noi da~i mai? (krab/kha)
- I would like to order food – Chan/Phom yak jansang aa ha~n noi (krab/kha)
- What do you recommend? – Khun yaak nae nam a rai? (krab/kha)
- Could I get the bill, please? – Chan/Phom kor kit ngern noi da~i mai? (krab/kha)
- Do you accept credit cards? – Khun rap but kray dit mai? (krab/kha)
- Can I have a bottle of water, please? – Chan/Phom kor na~m kuuat neung noi dai mai? (krab/kha)

❖ Can I have some ice, please? – Chan/Phom kor na~m kaeng noi da~i mai? (krab/kha)

Safety Note: When requesting ice in Thailand, ensure it's made from bottled or filtered water, as the tap water may not be safe to drink. This caution helps avoid potential health issues while enjoying your stay.

❖ I'm searching for the bus terminal – Chan/Phom gam lang haa sa taa nee kon song (krab/kha)

❖ Do you serve vegetarian meals? – Chan/Phom bpen Maleg sa wi rat khun mi ar ha~n Maleg sa wi rat mai? (krab/kha)

❖ This meal is overly spicy for me. – Ar ha~n nee mun ped gern bpai sam rap chan (krab/kha)

❖ Could you please give me the menu? – Chan/Phom kor may nu noi daai mai? (krab/kha)

❖ This seems a bit pricey, could you reduce it? – Mun raa ka~ soong bpai khun chuuay lod hai noi daai mai? (krab/kha)

❖ How do I get to the bus heading to...? – Chan/Phom ja keun rot bas bpai tee nai da~i ba~ng...? (krab/kha)

- ❖ I have allergies to… – Chan/Phom mai por jai tee… (krab/kha)
- ❖ Is it possible to have this without…? – Chan/Phom mai aow da~i mai…? (krab/kha)
- ❖ May I get a table for two, please? – Chan/Phom kor dto sam rap song kon noi da~i mai? (krab/kha)
- ❖ I don't know how to speak Thai – Chan/Phom poot Thai mai daai

ESSENTIAL THAI WORDS FOR TRAVELERS

For travelers, getting familiar with some essential Thai words will greatly aid in your journey for basic interactions.

- ❖ Yes – Chai (krab/kha)
- ❖ No – Mai (krab/kha)
- ❖ Food – Ar harn
- ❖ Water – Naam
- ❖ Beer – Beer
- ❖ Rice – Kaow
- ❖ Chicken – Gai
- ❖ Pork – Neuua moo
- ❖ Beef – Nueuua wuua

- ❖ Fish – Bplaa
- ❖ Vegetables – Pak
- ❖ Fruit – Pon la mai
- ❖ Tea – Chaa
- ❖ Coffee – Gaa fae
- ❖ Salt – Gleuua
- ❖ Spicy – Ped
- ❖ Not spicy – Mai ped
- ❖ Warm – Ron
- ❖ Cool – Yen
- ❖ Nice – Dee
- ❖ Not nice – Mai dee
- ❖ Large – Yaii
- ❖ Tiny – Lek
- ❖ Today – Wan nee
- ❖ Tomorrow – Prung nee
- ❖ Yesterday – Meuua waan
- ❖ Assistance! – Chuuay duuay
- ❖ Sweet – Waan
- ❖ Tasty – Aa roi
- ❖ Sweet treat – Kong waan
- ❖ Morning meal – Aa haan chao

- Noon meal – Meu tiiang
- Evening meal – Meu yen
- Shrine – Wat
- Thai boxing – Muay Thai
- Gallery – Pi pit ta pan
- Elephant – Chang

Interesting Fact: Chang is also the leading beer brand in Thailand. Don't miss trying it!

- Thai rubdown – Nuad paen thai
- Market on water – Dta laat naam
- Motorbike – Sa goot ter
- Outsider – Farang
- Entry – Taang kao
- Departure – Taang ork
- Cooling system – Kreuang bprap ar gart
- Restroom – Hong naam
- Pull – Deung
- Push – Plak
- Men – Poo chaai
- Women – Poo ying
- Location of...? – ... Yoo tee nai?

- Coach depot – Bpaai rot may
- Aerodrome – Sa nam bin
- Admission – Dtuua
- Festivity – Bpaa dtee
- Cash dispenser – Dtoo ay tee em
- Railway depot – Sa taa nee rot fai
- Cost – Ra kha
- Gratis – Free
- Plastic money – Bud kray dit
- Infirmary – Rohng pa ya baan
- Constabulary – Tam ruuat

USEFUL THAI GREETINGS

Greeting someone in Thai is a fantastic way to connect with locals or new acquaintances during a night out. Demonstrating an interest in their culture through these greetings can be very appreciated!

- How are you? – Sa baai dee mai (krab/kha)
- What is your name? – Khun cheu a rai (krab/kha)
- My name is... – Chan/Phom cheuu...... (krab/kha)
- Pleased to meet you – Yin dee tee dai roo jak (krab/kha)

- ❖ Where do you come from? – Khun ma jark tee nai? (krab/kha)
- ❖ I come from... – Chan/Phom ma jark ... (krab/kha)
- ❖ Good morning – Sa wat dee ya~m chao (krab/kha)
- ❖ Good afternoon – Sa wat dee dton bai (krab/kha)
- ❖ Good evening – Sa wat de~ dton yen (krab/kha)
- ❖ Good night – Raa dtree sa wat (krab/kha)

BASIC THAI NUMBERS

Even though English is widely spoken, especially in tourist areas, knowing Thai numbers is an excellent conversation starter.

- ❖ English - Thai
- ❖ Zero - Soon
- ❖ One - Neung
- ❖ Two - Song
- ❖ Three - Saam
- ❖ Four - See
- ❖ Five - Ha
- ❖ Six - Hok
- ❖ Seven - Jed
- ❖ Eight - Paed

- ❖ Nine - Gaow
- ❖ Ten - Sib

FREQUENTLY ASKED QUESTIONS ABOUT THAI PHRASES AND WORDS

- ❖ How do you say "Hello" in Thai?

"Hello" is said as "สวัสดี" (sawadee) in Thai. Men say "สวัสดีครับ" (sawadee krab) and women say "สวัสดีค่ะ" (sawadee kha) to be polite.

- ❖ How do you ask "How are you?" in Thai?

To ask "How are you?" in Thai, you say (sa ba~i dee mai?). Add "krab" for men and "kha" for women at the end, making it "sabaai dee mai krap?" or "sabaai dee mai kha?".

- ❖ How do you say "I love you...." in Thai?

"I love you...." in Thai is "ฉันรักคุณ..." (Chan rak khun....). For males, use "Pom rak khun" and females use "Chan rak khun" to make it gender-specific.

Learning Thai might seem daunting, but being able to communicate in the local language enhances the experience of navigating through Thailand. While many people in tourist spots speak English, speaking even a little Thai will immerse you deeper into the culture and is sure to be appreciated by the locals!

Conclusion and Final Thoughts

In the enchanting pages of "Krabi: A Journey Through Paradise," Alice John has not only shared her heart but also extended an exclusive invitation to wanderlust souls seeking adventures in the breathtaking landscapes of Krabi. This guidebook is more than just a collection of travel tips and stories; it's a secret map to the heart of paradise, carefully crafted to ensure your journey is nothing short of magical.

But, dear reader, as you turn each page and find yourself lost in the wonders of Krabi, there lies a hidden gem, a quiet request nestled between the lines. If the tales of towering cliffs, hidden lagoons, and the warmth of the local hospitality have touched your spirit, if Alice's journey has inspired you to embark on your own, then consider sharing the magic. Your thoughts, experiences, and reflections could be the guiding light for fellow travelers yearning to explore the beauty of Krabi.

By leaving a review, you're not just penning down your thoughts; you're becoming a part of a larger community of adventurers, a secret society of dreamers and explorers who rely on each other's wisdom to uncover the world's hidden wonders. Your insights will echo in the hearts of future readers, guiding them as they navigate their own paths through the enchanting realms of Krabi.

So, as you reach the end of your journey with "Krabi: A Journey Through Paradise," remember, your adventure has only just begun. Share your experience, leave a trail of stars as dazzling as the Bioluminescent plankton on a Krabi shore, and let your words be the beacon for others who, just like you, are on the verge of discovering their own paradise.

Alice John, in a whisper through the winds of Krabi, thanks you for your companionship on this journey. Your voice, dear traveler, is the secret ingredient to the continuing tale of Krabi. Let it be heard.

Printed in Great Britain
by Amazon

44193458R00076